DAILY
PRAYERS

Preachers, worship leaders and individuals will highly value how these short, godly prayers stimulate, encourage and structure our prayers. They give us words to use throughout the day as we lift our hearts and voices to God. The sketch of the life of F. B. Meyer, one of the major voices of British Christianity during the nineteenth and early twentieth centuries, will also inspire and equip leaders for shepherding congregations with pastoral wisdom and humility amidst great challenge.

Bryan Chapell
President, Covenant Theological Seminary, St Louis, Missouri

F.B. Meyer's Daily Prayers are a Christian devotional classic: short but substantial, biblical and beautiful, profound and piercing, realistic and hopeful. You will read them in seconds and think about them all day. You may find these brief prayers are just what you need to open your own heart up to the Lord and to prompt your communion with Him in prayer. I especially appreciate this edition, edited by Anne and David Calhoun. The biographical introduction is extremely helpful, and Dr. Calhoun's description of how he personally uses these prayers, with some examples of his notations, provides useful counsel for those wanting to benefit from this unique collection of petitions. I have recently started sharing these prayers on social media, and many have commented how encouraging, convicting and motivating they are. I am delighted that this solid spiritual help is once again available in print.

Ligon Duncan
Chancellor and CEO, Reformed Theological Seminary

DAILY PRAYERS

A SHORT PETITION
FOR EVERY DAY IN THE YEAR

BY

F. B. MEYER

EDITED
BY
ANNE AND DAVID CALHOUN

CHRISTIAN
HERITAGE

David B. Calhoun is Professor of Church History at Covenant Theological Seminary, St. Louis, Missouri. He studied with Francis Schaeffer and has led international ministry organisations in America and Europe. Among his writing credits is *Grace Abounding: The Life, Books and Influence of John Bunyan.*

Copyright © Christian Focus Publications

paperback ISBN 978-1-5271-0206-4
epub ISBN 978-1-5271-0192-0
mobi ISBN 978-1-5271-0193-7

10 9 8 7 6 5 4 3 2 1

Originally published in 1913 as *My Daily Prayers* by
Fleming H. Revell Company.
Republished in 1995 by Harold Shaw Publishers.

Published in 2007
Reprinted in 2018
in the
Christian Heritage Imprint
by
Christian Focus Publications, Ltd.,
Geanies House, Fearn, Ross-shire,
IV20 1TW, Great Britain.
www.christianfocus.com

Cover design by Daniel Van Straaten

Printed by Bell & Bain

A Sketch of the Life of
F. B. Meyer

by

David B. Calhoun

Early life

Frederick Brotherton Meyer was born on April 8 1847, to a well-to-do London businessman, Frederick Meyer, and his wife, Ann. Meyer's great grandfather, John Sebastian Meyer (named for Johann Sebastian Bach, a family friend), had migrated from Worms, Germany, to London in the early part of the eighteenth century. Meyer's grandmother on his mother's side was a Quaker poet whose work was praised by Sir Walter Scott.

F. B. Meyer could not pinpoint the exact time when he was 'converted,' a matter that caused him some concern until he heard Charles Haddon Spurgeon explain, in a sermon at the Metropolitan Tabernacle, that what mattered was for a person to be alive, even if his or her birth date had been forgotten. Ann Meyer remembered that when her son was about five years old, he prayed one Sunday evening the words 'Put thy Holy Spirit in me to make my heart good, like Jesus Christ was.' The little boy continued to pray this prayer every day.

In 1866 Meyer began studying for the ministry at Regent's Park College. In 1869 he graduated with a London University degree. On February 20 1871, he married Jane Eliza (Jeannie) Jones – a woman of 'fascinating personality, creative imagination, and undeviating will.' They had one daughter.

Churches in Richmond, Liverpool, and York

During his college training Meyer gathered and organized a Baptist church in Richmond, later named Duke Street Baptist Church. (Meyer's father, while he was a student in Edinburgh, had attended Charlotte Chapel, a Baptist church known for its strong evangelical preaching.) F. B. Meyer then served for two years as an assistant minister to C. M. Birrell at Pembroke Chapel in Liverpool. Mr Birrell said to him after he had preached one Sunday, 'Meyer, that was quite a good sermon you preached but it was a topical sermon. There will come a time when you will have spoken on all the topics. Where will you be then? You had better learn to expound the Word of God.' It was good advice, and Meyer carefully adhered to it for the rest of his life.

In 1872 F. B. Meyer was called to York to the Priory Street Baptist Church – in the shadow of York Minster, one of the grandest church buildings in the world. The young pastor met Dwight L. Moody and his associate and singer

Ira D. Sankey, when Moody's momentous British ministry began in June 1873 in York. Meyer was immediately drawn to Moody, whom he called 'a great and noble soul.' The friendship between Meyer and Moody lasted until the latter's death in 1899. Moody never forgot that Meyer was the first minister to welcome him heartily to England, and Meyer never forgot that he learned from Moody the art of winning men and women for Christ. Evangelism now became an essential part of Meyer's ministry. He sought to turn Priory Street Baptist Church into an agency for actively reaching the working classes with the gospel.

Leicester

In 1874 Meyer moved from York to Victoria Road Church in Leicester. After four years' ministry he resigned from Victoria Road but was persuaded to remain in Leicester as pastor of a new church, called Melbourne Hall. Melbourne Hall became a vigorous center for outreach and mercy ministries, and congregations quickly numbered 1,500, with 2,500 in Sunday school. Meyer personally was engaged in ministry to discharged prisoners, meeting with over 4,500 men and women, and began a firewood business and a window-cleaning service to provide employment for them.

Many people visited Melbourne Hall, including Hudson Taylor and two of 'the Cambridge Seven' who had volunteered for China – Stanley Smith and C. T. Studd. The visit of Smith and Studd in 1884 marked 'an epoch' in Meyer's life. Studd and Smith were nationally known sportsmen who, with five other Cambridge University students, were about to leave for missionary service in China. Meyer was impressed by the constant 'rest and strength and joy' that marked the two men. They told the young pastor, whose Christian life had been 'spasmodic and fitful,' that 'a man must not only believe in Christ for final salvation, but must trust Him for victory over every sin, and for deliverance from every care.' Meyer confessed that 'his early Christian life was marred and his ministry paralyzed' because he 'had kept back one thing from the bunch of keys he had given to the Lord.' He now experienced greater joy and freedom in his Christian life as he surrendered the last 'key' to the Lord and, 'for the first time,' he later explained, took the will of God as 'the sole aim' of his whole life.

London

F. B. Meyer served in two London churches for the next forty-one years. In 1888, he moved from Leicester to Regent's Park Chapel, an upper-class Baptist church in the west of London. There he found 'a united handful of people, a noble building, a glorious gospel, a divine Spirit.' Meyer loved London. He said that he could hear the 'music of the waves' when he walked by the River Thames. At Regent's Park Chapel Meyer achieved a national reputation. He was loved by Nonconformists throughout England and respected by a great many Anglicans.

In 1892, the year Spurgeon died, Meyer went from Regent's Park Chapel to Christ Church, Lambeth, one of the poorest areas of South London. Christ Church was a stately building near enough to Westminster Abbey to be considered 'the Cathedral of Nonconformity'. It was a nondenominational church, although loosely attached to Congregationalism, with a goal of embracing all sections of the Church of Christ – hence its name. This appealed to the Baptist pastor, who wanted, as he put it, to be 'equally in touch with all sections of Evangelical Christianity'.

Under F. B. Meyer's ministry, congregations at Christ Church grew from a few hundred to 2,500 on Sundays. There were 4,000 children and adults in the church's eight Sunday schools. Meyer was concerned 'to make Christ Church the home of the working people that thronged the adjacent streets.' He began a Sunday afternoon meeting, called the 'Brotherhood', which, in time, attracted 800 working-class men. Two corners in the church building, named 'Teetotal Corner' and 'Consecration Corner', were designated for those who wished to sign a total-abstinence pledge and for those who desired to become Christians. The men loved Meyer, calling him 'the skipper'. Meyer was leaving a beautiful Ontario church, during a visit to Canada years later, when a rough hand was suddenly thrust toward him, and a rugged man called, 'Hello, Skipper.' 'I can't tell you how my heart was thrilled by that name "skipper,"' Meyer told the church congregation that night. 'How I want to thank that dear man for calling me that! Oh, how I wish I could still do that work! Those crowds of rough workingmen, and drunkards, and men sick of life! I had

800 of them every Sunday afternoon, and, mind you, I never talked politics or economics, but always Jesus Christ, and there were conversions by the score.' Meyer also began a meeting for women – the Women's 'At Home' it was called – which met on Mondays.

During fourteen years of his London pastorates, Meyer devoted Saturday afternoons to a Bible class for young men in the Aldersgate Street YMCA Hall, teaching the International Sunday School Lesson. One of those young men was F. W. Boreham (later popular author and pastor in Australia), who remembered the meetings:

> I have often wondered how any man would get on nowadays who attempted to run a Bible class for young men on Saturday afternoons! But Dr Meyer did it, and every Saturday some hundreds of young fellows flocked to him at Aldersgate Street. I seem to see him now as he sat on his high stool at his table below us – for the seats sloped up from him – pouring out to us the treasures of his deep experience. Every now and again he would become excited by his theme and, with an 'Oh, my brothers I want to tell you,' he would leave the stool and with eyes sparkling and hands gesticulating, would pace up and down the floor before us. I really think that we lived for those Saturday afternoons.

Theology

F. B. Meyer was passionately committed to evangelical distinctives – the authority of the Bible, the cross of Christ, personal conversion, and active Christian service (especially overseas missions).

Two theological traditions shaped his early thinking: Quaker spirituality, inherited through his mother's family, and, more important, Calvinism.

Meyer read the nineteenth-century Scottish Presbyterians such as Andrew and Horatius Bonar, W. C. Burns, and Robert Murray McCheyne. One of his most treasured possessions was a page from McCheyne's diary. Meyer admired Richard Baxter's 'divine passion,' Jonathan Edwards' preaching, which he described as 'logic on fire,' and the missionary zeal of David Brainerd and Henry Martyn. Meyer softened what he believed were the divisive elements of Calvinism and in general played down the importance of creeds.

Meyer's emphasis in theology was direct, personal communion with God – a theology of the heart. The mystic strain in Meyer was developed by his study of Francis of Assisi, John Tauler, Brother Lawrence, and Madame Guyon, as well as by Walter Marshall's *The Gospel Mystery of Sanctification* and the writings of William Law and John Wesley.

In the Downgrade Controversy that troubled Baptist life in England during the 1880s, Meyer attempted to hold a moderate position. C. H. Spurgeon, minister of the five-thousand-member Metropolitan Tabernacle in London, had become increasingly concerned about theological trends in the Baptist denomination and, in October 1887, resigned from the Baptist Union. While agreeing with the 'main contention' of Spurgeon's protest, Meyer was committed to conciliation. He believed that the Baptist Union was 'sound at its heart,' despite the unfortunate 'chance utterances' of some of its ministers. Meyer tried to preserve unity by rejecting calls for a creedal basis for the Baptist Union on the grounds that the bond between Christians was life rather than doctrine. Baptists knew 'in heart,' he said, what was meant by the word 'evangelical.'

As a committed Baptist, Meyer held that believer's baptism by immersion was an important testimony to conversion and Christian commitment. He insisted that a facility for immersion be provided when he came to Christ Church. He encouraged members of other churches to receive believer's baptism, assuring them that they could still continue as members in their own churches. 'This rite is a personal matter between the Lord and the individual believer,' he maintained.

F. B. Meyer's major concerns and goals in ministry were evangelical unity, personal holiness, foreign missions, and social reform.

Evangelical Unity

Ian M. Randall calls F. B. Meyer 'the most important bridge builder in the evangelical world of his day.' By stressing practical application rather than doctrine, Meyer related in a way no one else did during his time 'to Churchmen and Nonconformists, to Calvinists and evangelicals of other persuasions.'

It was through the example of D. L. Moody that Meyer came to see 'a wider, larger life, in which mere denomination-alism could have no place.' Meyer prized the mystical unity of the whole church more than its outward form 'in broken bits' or denominations. While remaining a strong Baptist in his convictions – in 1906 he was elected to the presidency of the Baptist Union – Meyer worked hard to further accord among the Free Churches (Baptists, Congregationalists, and other Nonconformists, or non-Anglican Protestants) and to promote a measure of understanding and co-operation between Anglicans and Nonconformists. Meyer was twice president of the National Free Church Council. When he resigned from Christ Church in 1907, he received what he called a second ordination to wider ministry as a 'traveling bishop' of the Free Churches.

In a sermon on 'The Oneness of Believers,' preached in Rome in May 1907 at the World's Fifth Sunday School Convention, when he was elected president of the World's Sunday School Association, Meyer explained:

> I find in my own ministry that supposing I pray for my own little flock, 'God bless me, God fill my pews, God send me a revival,' I miss the blessing; but as I pray for my big brother, Mr Spurgeon, on the right-hand side of my church, 'God bless him,' or my other big brother, Campbell Morgan, on the other side of my church, 'God bless him,' I am sure to get a blessing without praying for it; for the overflow of their cups fills my little bucket.

When the Anglican bishop of Adelaide, Australia, refused to allow Meyer to conduct a meeting in Trinity Church, despite the fact that it had been advertised, Meyer responded by holding the service in a school and saying that he hoped one day 'to kneel before the throne of God with a high churchman on one side and a Quaker on the other.'

F. B. Meyer's request, in *My Daily Prayer*, for July 22 is for Christian unity: 'Have mercy, I pray, on all who call themselves Christians; lead them out of their wanderings and divisions so that people may see their unity in Jesus Christ and believe that you sent him to be the Redeemer of the world.'

Meyer's importance in British Christianity is seen in the choice of the three leading speakers at the Royal Albert Hall celebration of the tercentenary of the publication of the Authorized Version of the Bible in 1911: the Archbishop of Canterbury, the prime minister, and F. B. Meyer.

Personal Holiness

One of the more influential and theologically balanced of the nineteenth-century movements promoting Christian sanctification was a predominantly Anglican creation called *Keswick*, named after the town in the English Lake District where annual conventions were held from 1875 on. Handley Moule, a leading Keswick speaker and bishop of Durham from 1900, summarized Keswick teaching as 'a crisis with a view to a process.' Some evangelicals, such as Bishop J. C. Ryle of Liverpool, viewed the Keswick message as one-sided, arguing that 'in following holiness the true Christian needs personal exertion and work as well as faith.'

The first time F. B. Meyer was invited to speak at Keswick, he left a late-night preconvention prayer meeting in the large tent and went out of 'the little town with its dazzling lamps, and climbed the neighboring hill.' He believed that there he received the fullness of the Spirit. Years later he remembered that experience. 'As I write, the summer night is again casting its spell on me. The light clouds veil the stars and pass. The breath of the mountains leads me to yearn for a fresh intake of God's Spirit. May we not count on the Anointing Spirit to grant us a fresh infilling when we are led to seek it?'

Meyer did not follow the Wesleyan tradition of sanct-ification as a 'second grace' by which believers are made sinless. He stressed, rather, the importance of Christians entering into 'victory,' or experiencing the 'higher life,' not by human effort but by surrender and trust in the strength of Christ living in the believer. The victorious Christian was freed from known sin, though never in this life attaining sinless perfection. Sin was suppressed, not eradicated, with the Holy Spirit keeping the self-life in subjection.

F. B. Meyer found a spiritual home in the Keswick movement with its emphasis on the Christian life and interdenominational flavor. He spoke at twenty-six of the annual Keswick conventions and became Keswick's leading international representative.

In November 1902 Meyer visited Jamaica in the British West Indies and preached at the Keswick convention in the little mountain town of Mandeville. I lived in Mandeville for four years, when I was principal of Jamaica Bible College, and served on the Mandeville Keswick Council. One day, while looking at the old book that recorded the Keswick speakers through the years, I was surprised and delighted to find the signature of F. B. Meyer.

Foreign Missions
F. B. Meyer zealously promoted foreign missions – the Baptist Missionary Society and the London Missionary Society, as well as interdenominational 'faith' missions such as the Regions Beyond Missionary Union, the China Inland Mission (he was a close friend of Hudson Taylor), and North Africa Mission. He began the South London Missionary Training College and led the school from 1893 to 1896, when it was merged with the Regions Beyond Missionary College. In 1920 Meyer rededicated himself to spreading the gospel 'in heathen lands' and became director of the interdenominational Regions Beyond Missionary Union.

Social Reform
F. B. Meyer, a major Keswick teacher and missionary statesman, was also a strong advocate of social reform. He has been described by Ian Randall as 'the personification of the Nonconformist conscience.' Meyer believed that every

church and every Christian should help to 'right social wrongs' by promoting human dignity, equality, and freedom of conscience. Great revivals of religion, Meyer maintained, always created social and political reconstruction. He rejoiced that the 'humanitarian side' of the gospel was becoming prominent and searched for ways in which the gospel, as he put it, could be 'incarnated again' in the world. As we have seen, while he was pastor in Leicester, Meyer visited the prison each morning, taking the discharged men and women to a coffeehouse for breakfast. He was personally deeply generous and trusting. He knew that he could be deceived – and sometimes was – but he believed that 'it was far better to be let down occasionally than never to have the satisfaction of lending a helping hand.' He campaigned for temperance and then for total abstinence, giving up his well-liked glass of sherry for the cause. He was so successful that he received threats from some pub owners whose income was being threatened. He fought to close over seven hundred houses of prostitution.

Although Meyer never parted from his conviction that preachers should proclaim the central doctrines of the Christian faith, he advocated 'particular preaching' to apply the gospel to specific social issues. He believed that the state should help right 'the wrongs which make the few rich and the many poor.' Meyer challenged Christians to go beyond soup kitchens and blankets to a concern for justice for the poor. He was tireless in his efforts to improve the condition of women, including campaigning for better wages for women. He believed that women's suffrage 'has got to come.'

Meyer worked hard to promote world peace and disarmament during the years leading up to World War I, but he strongly supported the British government's declaration of war in 1914. The war was, in Meyer's opinion, the 'clearest, cleanest and most Christian war' Great Britain had ever fought. Although he supported the war, Meyer insisted that the rights of conscientious objectors be protected.

Premillennialism

Whereas some nineteenth-century evangelicals shared St Augustine's belief that there was no future millennium, most believed that the gospel would advance through the world until the establishment of an earthly golden age or millennium. Only after that period of peace and prosperity would the second coming of Christ take place. In the early nineteenth century, however, a different eschatological approach gained favor. Premillennialists believed that the second coming of Christ would inaugurate, not follow, the millennium. The shortness of time before the soon-expected end of the age gave to many Christians a heightened sense of significance to everyday life and an added urgency to evangelism. Leading evangelicals who espoused premillennialism were J. C. Ryle, the bishop of Liverpool; Horatius Bonar, one of the most influential ministers of the Free Church of Scotland; and Baptists C. H. Spurgeon and F. B. Meyer.

Decline in Christian influence after World War I caused a shift in F. B. Meyer's outlook. Although still urging evangelism and social improvement, he was not as optimistic as he had been during his early ministry. He now expected only a 'remnant' to form the true, faithful church. He called on evangelicals to look for the imminent return of Christ and the setting up of his millennial kingdom on earth. For the last dozen years of his life, Meyer was the leader of the Advent Testimony and Preparation Movement.

Travels

From D. L. Moody, Meyer received a vision for international ministry. He preached throughout Europe and made some twenty visits to the United States and Canada. Following the Welsh Revival of 1904–1905, Meyer reported in Los Angeles what he had observed in Wales, greatly encouraging future leaders of the infant Pentecostal movement. Robert G. Lee, later famous preacher of Bellevue Baptist Church in Memphis, Tennessee, heard Meyer give a chapel talk at Furman College in Greenville, South Carolina. That message, Lee wrote,

> enriched my life and inspired me immeasurably. I was having a difficult time financially – wondering how I could secure sufficient money for college expenses. On the particular morning when Dr Meyer – bright of eyes, white of hair, pleadingly earnest in voice – spoke to the students, he spoke to one young man who was in a mood something like that of Elijah under the juniper tree. … That morning,

Dr Meyer talked on something about the difficulties Moses met with in his leadership of the Children of Israel. He assured us that we, no matter what we did or where we went, could not expect to escape difficulties and problems beyond human abilities to solve. Then he put into my mind a statement which has been a constant source of courage, of strength, of wisdom, of faith, of daring to me. This is the statement: 'You never test the resources of God until you attempt the impossible.' Since that day, I have read all the books I could find by Dr Meyer. … His books have been a source of stimulation for my mind, of comfort for my heart, of encouragement in times when the roads were rough, the hills high, the valleys deep and dark.

Dr Meyer also preached in the West Indies, the Near East, India, China, South Africa, and Australia. In 1908 he spent six months in South Africa, where he was appalled by the government's policies toward black and colored people, and had respectful discussions with Mahatma Gandhi, who was at that time in South Africa. It is probable that Meyer personally addressed more of the worldwide evangelical and wider Christian community of his day than any other British minister.

Last Years
Dr Meyer's eightieth birthday was celebrated on April 8 1927. There were short speeches about his life – 'The Gladness of Spring,' 'The Glory of Summer,' 'The Fulfillment of Autumn,' and 'The Promise of Winter.' Meyer was given

a gift of £800. The next day, he took exquisite pleasure in dividing the money among many Christian works. In 1928 the *Sunday Express* of London published an article from F. B. Meyer – 'My Religion at 81' – in which he wrote, 'Probably it would have been easier to state my religious faith and outlook when I was eighteen than now when the figures are reversed. But knowing all that I know of the travail, the agony, and the heart-break; behind it all, through it all, dealing with it all – *God is Love.*'

During Dr Meyer's last preaching tour of Canada he said to a minister friend, 'I do hope my Father will let the river of my life go flowing fully till the finish. I don't want it to end in a swamp.'

F. B. Meyer died on March 28 1929, in a nursing home in Bournemouth. His beloved wife, Jeannie, had died in the same home a few weeks earlier. They had been devoted companions for more than fifty-eight years. The day before he died, a friend asked if Meyer had any new vision of his Savior. 'No,' he replied, 'just the constant interchange between Him and me.'

At his funeral service on April 3 at Christ Church in London, the 'Hallelujah Chorus' ended the service – it was Dr Meyer's one request. The music ceased; the congregation joined in the *Nunc Dimittis*. Meyer was buried in Bournemouth, where two thousand people gathered. In the graveside service it was suggested that an appropriate memorial to F. B. Meyer would read, 'Here lies a man that reckoned on God.' Meyer himself often summed up his ministry with the words 'John did no miracle, but all that he spake of this Man was true.'

Writings

F. B. Meyer wrote over a hundred books and booklets, and by the time of his death in 1929 5 million copies were in print. Spurgeon commended Meyer's writings as 'not only spiritual … but also thoughtful, fresh, … and thoroughly practical.' Next to Spurgeon's, the writings of Meyer were the most popular devotional books in Sweden. In Stockholm the Swedish queen greeted him warmly, saying, 'I look upon you as an old friend, as I have read your books.'

Meyer's broad appeal is understood when we read the opening words of his *Bible Commentary*. This work, wrote Meyer, is for 'busy people, students, business-men, Sunday school workers and older scholars, soldiers and sailors, [and] people on the hills and on the prairies, living on the edge of the great tides of human activity.' His goal was to help everybody read through the entire Bible – 'the true way to know the Bible is to read it through from beginning to end' – and to read it 'not only with our head, but with our heart,' asking the Holy Spirit 'to unlock and unfold its sacred mysteries.'

My Daily Prayer

Years ago I came across a small (three inches by four inches) book of prayers by F. B. Meyer. I have used these brief prayers of a sentence or two many times. The little black-covered book has come apart, but I have preserved it and treasure all the pages. In the margins I have noted a number of critical events in my life next to the prayer for that day. Beside January 8 are the words 'A great disappointment.' The prayer I prayed from F. B. Meyer that day was: 'Fill me with your joy, Lord, so that I may have much to give to my family and friends and to the great, sad world around me. Keep me from hiding my light under the basket of my own anxieties.' April 24 has my words 'A friend is dying' beside the prayer: 'Most gracious God, wherever, at this hour, there is serious sickness in home or hospital, wherever souls are passing from time into eternity, wherever there are anguish, peril and alarm, may your gentle Holy Spirit pour out peace and help.' The next day I prayed: 'Blessed Lord, hear me for those I love, especially for the ones who are passing through the Valley of the Shadow, or to whom the day brings no alleviation of pain or sorrow. Put gladness into their hearts, may light shine in their darkness, and let the days of their mourning be ended.' Next to December 27, I have written the words 'First chemotherapy.' And I prayed: 'Blessed Lord, may I be strong not for myself alone, but for others. Teach me to bear the infirmities of the weak, to support those that are overborne in the fight of life, and to lighten the load of care beneath which many of my fellow believers are pressed to the earth.' Recently, after a difficult experience with fungal and bacterial pneumonia, I was diagnosed with a serious heart problem. It seemed too much. I went back to my office from the doctor and turned to *My Daily Prayer*, where I read these words: 'King of Love, let the leaves of the Tree of Life be for my healing, and let your peace settle down, like the evening calm, on my harassed nature.' Again and again I have found the words to pray in Meyer's little book, and again and again God has answered those prayers.

These prayers are scripture based and scripture enriched, often using the very words of scripture and always following the teaching of the Bible. By use of these prayers, one may learn how to pray in deeper, more profound, more scriptural language.

The prayers center in the worship of God. In a few words we are led to the Father, Son, and Holy Spirit, with appropriate biblical descriptions of the Holy Trinity.

The prayers concentrate our petitions usually – but not always – on personal holiness. This is, of course, one of the great themes of the Bible and should be the heart's desire of every Christian. 'If I had cherished iniquity in my heart, the Lord would not have listened,' the Psalmist wrote (Ps. 66:18). We need to pray for pure hearts so that we may pray for more than that. Then we can move from prayers for ourselves to prayers for others. The prayer for February 26 includes all members of God's 'great scattered family' and asks God to 'satisfy the desire of every living thing.' On March 2 we pray for 'the lonely and sad-hearted, the forsaken and forgotten, the sinful and miserable.' For March 30 the prayer is for 'our leaders and the rulers of other lands; for statesmen, judges, magistrates, and all in authority.' The prayer for July 2 remembers those 'who have met with accident and sudden sorrow' and those 'who are lonely, and desolate, and forlorn.' This prayer invites us to add names of people we know whose needs are set forth in these words. On July 10 we are led to pray for God's 'missionary-servants.' Again, specific names come to mind as we pray that prayer. The prayer for November 22 requests help for 'those who teach, or write books, or edit newspapers.'

These little prayers may develop into longer prayers as, following the theme of each prayer, we add our own thoughts and petitions. One way to expand the prayers is to pray for someone else the same prayer that you have just prayed for yourself. Think of someone, a family member or friend, or someone you know or have heard about, for whom you can pray today's prayer. In this way we follow our Lord's instructions to pray in the plural – '*Our* Father ... give *us* this day *our* daily bread, and forgive *us* our debts ... and lead *us* not into temptation, but deliver *us* from evil.'

The language of most of the prayers has been slightly altered to conform to modern style. Some of the prayers have been changed more substantially to provide greater clarity and usefulness while preserving the themes and flavor of the originals.

For further information about F. B. Meyer's life, see Bob Holman, *F. B. Meyer: If I Had a Hundred Lives* (Christian Focus, 2007); W. Y. Fullerton, *F. B. Meyer: A Biography* (Marshall, Morgan & Scott, 1929) and Ian M. Randall, *Spirituality and Social Change: The Contribution of F. B. Meyer (1847–1929)* (Paternoster Press, 2003).

January

January 1

*B*e with me, Lord, as I step out on the untrodden way of this new year. I do not know what it may bring of joy or sorrow, of temptation or service; but I humbly commit myself and my way to you. Make the best that you can of me for your glory.

January 2

I thank you, O Son of God, that there is no need for me to go up to heaven to bring you down, or into your grave to bring you up. You are here, in this hour and at this place. I confess you as Lord and believe in my heart that you are risen from the dead.

January 3

You have said, Lord Jesus, that anyone who believes in you has everlasting life. I do now believe. With my whole heart I look to you as Savior, Friend, and King. I receive from your hand not only life, but life more abundantly.

January 4

Deliver me, my Lord and Master, from self-confidence, self-centeredness, and self-consciousness. May you be my confidence and the center of my life. May I always be more conscious of your presence than of the presence or absence of others.

January 5

Fix my heart, Lord, on you, that during the changes and chances of life I may be kept steadfast and unmovable and always doing your work.

January 6

Lord Jesus, you know the weakness of my human nature. Take away from me the fear of death; and when I come to the end of my earthly life, open for me the beautiful gate so that I may pass through it into the eternal home of God.

January 7

*L*ord, it is not in ourselves to direct our ways. I pray that I may never lean on my own understanding but trust you with all my heart. May I be led in the way everlasting.

January 8

*F*ill me with your joy, Lord, so that I may have much to give to my family and friends and to the great, sad world around me. Keep me from hiding my light under the basket of my own anxieties.

January 9

Help me, dear Lord, to walk in the footsteps of your holy life – denying myself and becoming poor so that those around me may be made rich. Teach me how to gain by giving, and to find by losing, as you have said in your Word.

January 10

My heart, O God, is broken and crushed for all the sins and failures of my life. I can only bring my heart to you as my best sacrifice, and I thank you for your promise not to despise it.

January 11

*M*ake me, blessed Master, strong in heart, full of courage, fearless of danger, holding pain and peril cheap when they lie in the path of duty. May I be strengthened by your Spirit.

January 12

*A*lmighty God, send your gospel around the world so that all nations may hear its glorious message; and may your strayed flock come to the one fold and the one Shepherd, your only begotten Son.

January 13

*B*y day and by night, in life and in death, may I trust you, O Lover of my soul, my ceaseless Friend, my unchangeable Savior. Into your hands I commit myself.

January 14

I turn to you, merciful God! To whom else could I go? My sins are many, but your mercy is great. My sins come quickly, but your anger is slow. My tears are bitter, but your tenderness is sweet and sure. May your gentleness make me great.

January 15

*D*ear God, my Father, to you nothing is small and nothing great. The ages are as sands on the shore and nations as drops in a bucket. Help me to look not at this affliction, which is but for a moment, but to the far greater and eternal weight of glory.

January 16

*G*rant me, Lord, I pray, a keen sensitiveness to all that is beautiful in nature and lovely in other people, so that I may see your beauty everywhere and become more like you.

January 17

*M*ake me, divine Friend, strong and pure in my friendships so that I may never break down boundaries that I ought to maintain, or withhold that which I ought to give for the help and comfort of others.

January 18

*D*ear Jesus, you were tempted in all ways as we are but did not sin. Give me grace to be watchful against the earliest and most insid-ious approaches of temptation, so that I may at once hide myself under the shadow of your wings.

January 19

*O*pen to me, Spirit of Truth, the treasures of your holy Word, so that I may continually be enriched and overflow with good words and works.

January 20

*G*racious Giver of all things, enable me to remember that all that you have given is a sacred trust to be held and used for others. At the end of my life, may I know that I have glorified you on the earth and finished the work you gave me to do.

January 21

Teach me to love your own beautiful world as you, to whom the mountains, flowers, and birds ministered, loved it. Speak to me through all the voices of nature, and grant me a quick sensitiveness to your presence everywhere.

January 22

Keep me, holy Savior, from all filthiness of the spirit as well as of the flesh, so that I might always seek to be holy as you are holy.

January 23

*M*ost wonderful Comforter, weary not of me who often wearies of myself. My only hope is in your love, which loves to the uttermost. Come once again and wash my soiled life. I thank you that you will not quench the smoking flax nor break the bruised reed.

January 24

*M*ay I never profess more than I actually experience, but may the hidden things of my heart be richer and fuller and deeper than I express to any but to you, O Searcher of hearts.

January 25

Come to me, Lord, in my sadness and brokenness. My fair ideals are like trampled flowers, and my attempts after perfection have failed. Do for me what I cannot do for myself, and perfect that which concerns me, because your mercy endures forever.

January 26

Deliver me, Lord, from every false way, so that I may cling to you with a perfect heart and, by your mercy, may know you, as also I am known of you through Jesus Christ.

January 27

*B*e my ruler and guide, gracious Father. I ask that in passing through temporal things I may not lose the eternal things.

January 28

*E*nrich me, my Lord, by the gifts of your Holy Spirit, so that I, patiently enduring the darkness of this world, and being filled with your heavenly grace, may become a burning and shining light until the day dawn and the shadows flee away.

January 29

*H*elp me to deny myself and be crucified to the world, so that I may follow the Lamb wherever he goes, holding up my head with joy because the day of my complete redemption draws near.

January 30

*B*y your holy illumination, Lord, enlighten my thinking, direct my heart and mind, keep my lips, and show yourself to me in the riches of your grace.

January 31

Teach me always, O Lord, to discern your will and to faithfully and diligently perform it, so that I may live to your glory.

FEBRUARY

February 1

*G*ive, Lord, to me and all your saints fullness of joy from your presence and treasures of goodness from your right hand.

February 2

*H*eavenly Father, we pray that Jesus Christ may become dearer to us. May we love him as a personal friend and hide ourselves in the hourly consciousness of his presence. May we have no taste or desire for things that he would disapprove. Let his love compel us not to live for ourselves, but for him.

February 3

Strengthen my faith, dear Lord, deepen my love, and accomplish in me all your good purpose.

February 4

Lord Jesus, do in me what you need to do so that you can do through me what you want to do.

February 5

*H*eavenly Vine! Pour your life through me so that I may bear much fruit for your sake.

February 6

*M*ost holy God, in whose sight the very heavens are unclean, do not spare me until my heart is washed, purified, and made clean, so that I may not seem better to others than I am.

February 7

*H*elp me so to live that those especially associated with me, and directing or serving me day by day, may long to have the love and joy that they see in me.

February 8

I am not my own; I give myself to you. Make of me as much as possible for your sake.

February 9

I long to place my will on your side. My God, keep it there, so that I may hate what you hate, love what you love, and do what you call me to do.

February 10

*G*ive me, most gracious Lord, singleness of heart, so that in every word, thought, and act I may put you first, and, in humility and integrity, seek to serve you and you only.

February 11

Give me, Heavenly Father, I pray, a self-forgetful spirit, so that I may be more anxious to give than to receive, more eager to understand than to be understood, more thoughtful of others, more unmindful of myself.

February 12

Teach me, Lord, when to speak and when to be silent; when to act and when not to act; and, in all the details of daily life, to do your will on earth as it is done in heaven.

February 13

*I*f this day I should get lost in the perplexities of life and the rush of many duties, search me out, gracious Lord, and bring me back into the quiet of your presence.

February 14

*G*ive me grace, my Father, that I may persevere in the work to which you have called me, not leaving it half done, nor giving up when the first enthusiasm has faded, or when other interests arise to attract me.

February 15

*C*alm me, O God, when my spirit is feverish and hot. Place your cool hand on my head, and breathe your peace through my heart. May I know that around my restlessness you are rest.

February 16

*M*ake me, holy Father, quick to respond to the pruning of the silver knife of your internal dealings with my soul, and sustain me under the iron knife of external pain.

February 17

*O*heavenly Father, help me to understand the sweet mystery and beauty of that name of yours – Abba Father.

February 18

*M*ay I so yield myself to you, as you wrestle with and overcome my proud nature, that, like Jacob, I may be enabled to prevail 'with God and man.'

February 19

O Jesus, who was meek and lowly in heart, may I be genuinely humble with the humility that does not realize that it is humble.

February 20

T each me to be as glad for the successes of others as for my own.

February 21

*F*ill me, I pray, with an absorb-ing passion for your kingdom, so that I may be eager for you to be glorified though I die unrecognized and unknown.

February 22

*H*elp me to believe that all things come from you, and that you have a plan for my life of which each passing incident is a part.

February 23

*M*ay I give not things only, but myself, to others, 'with full measure, heaped up, and running over.' May I despair of no one, and look for nothing in return.

February 24

I bring to you, O Lord, my desires and pray that you would cleanse them by the searching fires of your pure Spirit, so that I may want those things only that you have chosen and prepared for me.

February 25

*E*ternal God, work in me 'not only to will but to do of your good pleasure'; and may I work out what you work in.

February 26

*H*eavenly Father! Take into your loving care my home, my loved ones far and near, and all members of your great scattered family. Let me not be anxious about tomorrow's provision or path, but trust you to provide and lead. Open your hand and satisfy the desire of every living thing.

February 27

*M*y Father, give me a simpler and more confiding faith. May I trust more than I know, and believe more than I can see; and when my heart is overwhelmed, lead me to the Rock that is higher than I.

February 28

*S*end me, gracious Lord, the Comforter; may He fill my life as rain fills dry places. May the parched ground of my heart become a garden. Instead of the thorn may there come up the fir tree, and instead of the briar, the myrtle.

MARCH

March 1

*B*lessed Lord, as far as it lies in my power may I live peaceably with all people. Teach me to commit my cause to you who judges righteously, not anxious to defend or avenge myself, but always more eager to be patient than to demonstrate the strength of my cause.

March 2

*L*ord God Almighty! Look on those to whom the world is dark. Send a ray of light to gladden the lonely and sad-hearted, the forsaken and forgotten, the sinful and miserable. And teach me how to comfort them with the comfort with which you have comforted me.

March 3

O Savior who seeks those who are lost until you find them, teach me to minister to the needs of others. May I have pity for those who do not know you and whose lives are one long outrage of your forbearing love. Give me something of your compassion and long-suffering.

March 4

M y Father God! Let the motto of my life be 'Glory to God in the highest,' for only so can there be peace in my heart and goodwill toward others. May my heart sing the angels' song.

March 5

*L*et a watch, O Lord, at the door of my lips, so that I may speak nothing inconsistent with truth and love.

March 6

*G*racious God, enable me to trace the rainbow of hope above the dark storm clouds that brood over my life; and may I rest confidently on that covenant, ordered in every detail and sure, which was sealed by the precious blood of Christ.

March 7

*K*ing of Glory and Lord of Hosts, who ascended in triumph to the right hand of the Father, leave me not comfortless, but come to me in your Holy Spirit, who is the Spirit of Truth.

March 8

*A*s Jesus my Lord ascended to heaven, enable me also, in heart and mind, to ascend to heaven and with him continually dwell.

March 9

May your love be so shed abroad in my heart, Lord, that I may always seek the things that are above where Christ sits at your right hand.

March 10

Help me, Father, to add to my faith, strength; and to strength, knowledge; and to knowledge, self-control; and to self-control, endurance; to endurance, godliness; and to godliness, kindness; and to kindness, love.

March 11

*T*each me not only to bear, but to love, your cross, Lord Jesus. And as I take and carry it, may I find that it is carrying me.

March 12

*G*rant me concentration of purpose and singleness of heart, so that I may do not many things, but much. Strengthen my heart to fear and serve you.

March 13

*H*eavenly Father, have mercy on those who do not know you. Take from them all ignorance, hardness of heart, and contempt of your Word; bring them home to your fold, so that they may be saved and become one flock under the Great Shepherd and Bishop of Souls.

March 14

*A*lmighty God, raise me from the death of sin to a life of righteousness by that same power that brought the Lord Jesus from the dead. May I walk in newness of life in the power of his resurrection.

March 15

*H*eavenly Father, I know that all things are working together for my good; but help me to wait patiently and work diligently, though the waiting be long and the toil hard.

March 16

O Lord, there is nothing in me that can attract or hold your love. I have failed often, and cost you much. Forgive my bitter past, and make me beautiful in the beauty which you will place upon me.

March 17

Heavenly Father, I thank you for the trials and pains that are always working for my good so that I can share your holiness. May I receive the fullness of your abundant grace.

March 18

Most gracious God, quicken me by your Holy Spirit, I pray, so that I may run in the way you have marked out for me. And may I always be kept looking to Jesus.

March 19

*H*oly Father, I thank you for your forgiving, merciful love. I gratefully realize that my sin cannot alter your love, though it may dim my enjoyment of it. Set me free from the love of sin so that it may not darken the light of your face.

March 20

*S*avior, may I be permitted not only to touch the hem of your garment, but to lean on your heart. Cause me to love you with all my heart.

March 21

*H*eavenly Father, make me like him who, though He was rich, yet for our sakes became poor so that many, through his poverty, might be made rich. Help me to deny myself and give joy and comfort to those less favoured than I am; and may I learn how much more blessed it is to give than to receive.

March 22

*A*mid the temptations of the Evil One and the aggravation of the ungodly, help me to stay steadfast and immovable, always abounding in the work of the Lord, remembering that in the Lord my labor is not in vain.

March 23

*M*ay the Holy Spirit bring to my remembrance the gracious words of Christ, whenever in the heat of passion or the stress of life I am tempted to forget them.

March 24

*W*hen temptation is near, may I meet it as a soldier who is conscious that the captain is fighting for me and with me.

March 25

*W*ithdraw my soul, I pray, from the absorbing delights of this world, with their petty aims and ideals, and open my eyes to the great joy of my inheritance in Christ.

March 26

*H*oly Spirit, teach me to put away anger, wrath, malice, and evil speech, loveless words and loveless acts. Give me, as your elect, a heart of compassion, kindness, humility, meekness, long-suffering. May I be patient and forgive others, as you bear with me and forgive me.

March 27

*H*asten the coming of your kingdom, Lord, the fulfilment of your promise, and the consummation of your purpose, so that the travail of this world may give way to the rest of your eternal Sabbath.

March 28

*L*ord Jesus, teach me to see the good in hard things, to discern the silver edge of lowering clouds, and to believe in your love that is leading me safely and by a right way to my home.

March 29

*H*eavenly Father! You kill and make alive. You bring down to the grave and bring up from the grave. You raise up the poor from the dust and lift the needy from despair, to make them sit in heavenly places and inherit the throne of glory. I praise you, O most High!

March 30

*L*ord Jesus, as you loved Jerusalem, teach me to love my country in a proper way. I pray for our leaders and the rulers of other lands; for statesmen, judges, magistrates, and all in authority, that we may be quietly and rightly governed, and that peace and happiness, truth and justice, faith and piety, may be established among us.

March 31

I would not hide nor cover my sins from you, Almighty God, my Heavenly Father, but confess them with a humble, repentant, and obedient heart. Forgive me, because of your goodness and mercy.

*A*PRIL

April 1

*M*ost wonderful Lord! Have mercy on those who have rejected the invitation of your gospel, to whom it has become 'a savor of death.' Bless those to whom it has become 'a fragrance of life.' Strengthen those who have missed church and communion because of sickness, bereavement, or for some other cause known to you.

April 2

*G*racious God, I thank you for the gift of your Holy Spirit, the Comforter – pure as dew, cleansing as fire, tender and refreshing as the breath of spring. Blessed Trinity, always giving your choice things to us, your unworthy children, accept my gratitude for which I have no words.

April 3

*M*ay my heart be so childlike and pure that I see the beauty of the world around me as it appears to the angels and as it appeared to you, Lord, when you looked at the lilies and birds.

April 4

*M*ay I not only find forgiveness in your cross, dear Lord, but may your forgiveness create in me rivers of living water, as the rod of Moses drew water from the rock.

April 5

*H*eavenly Father, help me to remember that what you have given you will also require. Enable me so to live that I may multiply the talents with which you have entrusted me, by using them for your sake and for the comfort and help of others.

April 6

*S*avior, may I unload your ships as they come, richly freighted, for my need. May I be glad for all the good you send and receive what is appropriate to life and godliness, so that my character may shine like gold, silver, and precious stones.

April 7

*O*h, to be wholly yours! To have no thought closed from your Spirit, no act other than what you approve, no word inconsistent with your perfect love, no purpose in which you cannot have a part.

April 8

*M*ay I be satisfied with talking or thinking about your love. Give me the grace to express it not only in great crises, but in petty annoyances and the daily fret.

April 9

*H*elp me to think more intently about your humility and patience, my Savior, so that almost unconsciously these traits may reappear in my own character.

April 10

*H*oly Father! In you everything is found that can make your children glad, and I praise you. You have kept me while I slept, I have awoken in safety, and to you I would consecrate my renewed strength. May the expressions of my heart, this morning, be joyful.

April 11

I pray, Lord, that you would give me a ready sympathy with others so that I may look at things from their standpoint and see myself as they see me.

April 12

*S*how me, today, dear Lord, one of your little ones to whom I can give a cup of cold water in your name.

April 13

*L*et me not dwell on the past, my Father, as though it held the best. May I dare to believe that the best is yet to be, and that you are filling my life with the rain of tears that will one day yield the wine of joy.

April 14

*L*ord Jesus, we thank you that a new day affords another opportunity for commitment and devotion. You have turned a fresh page in my life's story. It comes from you without blemish or soil; help me to keep it so. Forgive the past blotted with my failures and sins, and help me to walk in paths of righteousness for your name's sake.

April 15

*M*ake me, Lord, to know the hope of your calling, the riches of the glory of your inheritance to the saints, and your amazing grace and power toward us who believe.

April 16

*H*elp me, Father, to appreciate the depth of your love. May I not disappoint you by using exaggerated outward expressions of that which is slowly growing in the relationship between you and me.

April 17

*L*ord, I cannot hope to sit on your right or your left in your kingdom, but permit me to sit at your feet and hear your Word.

April 18

*F*ather, we know that you do suffer in our suffering, and that your sympathy is quick and tender and deep. We thank you that Jesus Christ has wept human tears and carried the weight of human sorrow. May we comfort others with the comfort by which we ourselves have been comforted by God.

April 19

*M*ake yourself so real to me that my first thought in everything will be to do your will and to avoid whatever might give you sorrow.

April 20

*L*et me not be satisfied with refraining from sin; but, as I live in you, may I bear the fruits of the Spirit, which are love, joy, and peace.

April 21

*M*ay I be quick to discern in each person I meet how I can help you in liberating that soul still further from the grave of sin and lifting it to a life of righteousness.

April 22

*H*eavenly Father! Forgive our sins and failures, and cleanse us from all evil for the sake of Jesus Christ, our Lord. Accept us graciously, and love us freely. May we hate sin as you do, and may your grace sink deeper into our hearts, purifying even the motives of thought and action.

April 23

Teach me, my Savior, to understand the meaning of your cross
that, dying to myself, I may enter
with you into the fullness of life.

April 24

Most gracious God,
wherever, at this hour,
there is serious sickness in home or
hospital, wherever souls are passing
from time into eternity, wherever
there are anguish, peril and alarm,
may your gentle Holy Spirit pour out
peace and help. I ask it in the name
of Jesus.

April 25

*B*lessed Lord, hear me for those I love, especially for the ones who are passing through the Valley of the Shadow, or to whom the day brings no alleviation of pain or sorrow. Put gladness into their hearts, may light shine in their darkness, and let the days of their mourning be ended.

April 26

O send your light and truth, and let them lead and bring me at last to my Father's house.

April 27

*M*ake me a bright Christian, I pray, not morbid and austere and silent, not foolish and frivolous, but radiant, glad, and making others happy.

April 28

*H*oly Father, give me grace to lay aside the works of darkness and put on the armor of light. May all self-indulgence, all that is earthly, selfish, and unholy, be put away, and may I not fail you in times of temptation.

April 29

Give me, my Father, a loving and thankful heart. May your mercies, like cords, bind me to yourself. Let nothing be held back from you; but make me like a palace of which every room is freely open to its Lord.

April 30

Heavenly Father, help me to consider the interests of others and to act kindly and generously towards them, because we are all your children and your limitless resources are at our command. Make me a blessing to those with whom I come in contact, so that I may touch their lives with traces of that uncreated light that I have caught from the face of Christ.

MAY

May 1

I pray, Lord, deliver me from the fear of death. When my eyes open in heaven, may I see you and hear your 'Well done.'

May 2

*K*eep me throughout this day from all that would grieve your Holy Spirit. Help me to look not on the dark clouds, but on your rainbow; not on the stormy waters, but on the face of Jesus; not on what you have taken or withheld, but on what you have given; not on my fickle and changeful heart, but on your love, which is steadfast as the great mountains.

May 3

For all your blessings, Heavenly Father, known to me, and for all unknown, accept my thanks. May I not murmur at your providence, or dread the future. Whatever happens, help me to believe in your unfailing care and to know that in the Valley of the Shadow you are by my side.

May 4

Help me never to reject your will, my God, or to complain that your discipline is too severe.

May 5

*M*ay I not want to be known by others for my faith or endurance, but only to you who sees in secret and rewards openly.

May 6

*K*eep me from running here and there for human sympathy. May I be satisfied with your care. Whom do I have in heaven but you, and on earth none is to be desired but you.

May 7

I pray today, Lord, that you will give me your Holy Spirit in greater measure, so that your saving presence may cleanse my conscience and enlighten my heart.

May 8

Take from my heart, Heavenly Father, I pray, all envy, jealousy, and everything that would cause a breach between me and others. Let nothing prevent the inflowing of your love to my heart, and its outflowing to others.

May 9

*S*ince it is your will, my God,
that I should suffer, give me
patience, gentleness, and forgetful-
ness of myself, and help me to
minister joy and good to others.

May 10

*G*ive me grace, Heavenly Father,
properly to use for the benefit
of other people those gifts with
which I am entrusted, so that I may
be a good steward of your mercies
and not be ashamed before you at
your coming.

May 11

*L*et me not hesitate to come to you, even when some shameful fall is fresh. May I dare to believe in your immediate forgiveness and restoration to your presence.

May 12

*L*ord, my love is like some feebly glimmering spark; I wish that it were like a hot flame. Kindle it by your breath till your love constrains me!

May 13

I pray, gracious Lord, that I may not miss any of those lessons that you want to teach me by your Spirit, your Word, and your providence.

May 14

*H*elp me, Father, to believe that what seem to be my losses are really gains, and that each ounce of affliction is adding to the weight of glory – not only in heaven, but now.

May 15

Keep me, Heavenly Father, as the apple of your eye; defend me by your power; hide me secretly in your pavilion from the strife of tongues and the fiery darts of the wicked one; and may the Holy Spirit so fill me with Christ my Lord that there may be no room for anything inconsistent with love.

May 16

May I not be so absorbed in my own concerns as to be indifferent to the innocent joys of children and others.

May 17

*L*ord! I pray, teach me to follow where you go and to sit at your feet and learn from you.

May 18

I ask, gracious Lord, to be kept watchful and alert, so that I may discern each movement of your hand and detect your will and guidance in the providence of little things.

May 19

*L*et me turn to you, Father, from the sweetest of earthly joys, to find that you are best of all, the fairest of ten thousand, and altogether lovely.

May 20

I draw near to you, all-powerful and ever-living God, in the name of your Son, Jesus Christ, my high priest and mediator who has passed into the heavens, where he lives to make intercession for sinners. Forgive and accept me for his sake.

May 21

*T*urn again my captivity, O Lord,
as the streams in the south.
Heal my backslidings, and do not
take your Holy Spirit from me.

May 22

*O*Lord Jesus Christ, grant me
such communion with you
that my soul may continually be
thirsty for that time when I shall
see you face to face in your glory.
Meanwhile, may I see your glory
in the mirror of your Word and be
changed by it.

May 23

*H*elp me, Lord, daily to deny worldly and dishonorable affections and desires, so that there may arise in me a life of righteousness, by the grace of your quickening Spirit.

May 24

*T*each me to be content to do your will, not looking this way or that to compare myself with others, seek their commendation, or escape their censure. May your voice be my only law, your smile my only reward.

May 25

I wake early from the night and turn to you, O God, for the light; for your light is better than life; so I will praise you. Take my hand in yours, and make the crooked places straight and the rough places plain, so that your name may be honored in my conduct and conversation.

May 26

G rant to me, Lord, the blessedness of the one whom you choose and bring to yourself.

May 27

*M*y God, my heart is overwhelmed within me; lead me to the Rock that is higher than I. In the shadow of your wings I will make my refuge.

May 28

*Y*ou are light, and in you is no darkness at all. I thank you for eyes to see, a heart to love, and a nature to enjoy your good and perfect gifts. I worship you, Father of Lights, in whom is no variableness, neither shadow of turning. Make light my darkness, I pray.

May 29

*S*ustain me, by your strong arm, as I walk in the mists and darkness of the valley, and may I know that your goodness and mercy follow me.

May 30

*C*ome Lord, I humbly pray, and clean my feet, my hands, and my lips from stains of flesh and spirit. Teach me to live a holy life in the fear of the Lord.

May 31

O my Savior, I am overtired and weary. The strain of my life has exhausted me. The pressure of daily business has robbed me of vitality. I have no strength left. Forgive me for my lack of simple, child-like faith. Come near and refresh me. Take the burden I cannot bear. Hush the fears I cannot quiet. Wipe the tears I cannot keep back.

JUNE

June 1

*M*ay I not faint under your loving discipline, Father, but accept it humbly and trustfully, so that I may share in your holiness.

June 2

I humbly ask that I may be so encouraged throughout this day with thoughts of you that this earthly life may be brightened with the spirit of heaven, and that I may go about my business as one who has seen the face of God.

June 3

*M*ay your companion-ship be so real to me, my Lord, that I may never give way to loneliness.

June 4

*M*y desire and prayer is that I may be filled with your love. Pour your love in my heart by the Holy Spirit, to enable me to love my neighbor as myself.

June 5

*M*erciful Savior, help
me to pray for
your family scattered in all lands.
Surround them with tender care.
Keep them from harm and sin.

June 6

I open my life to let in your
fullness, Lord. My capacity is
small, and I pray that my heart may
be made large so that I may miss
nothing of your blessing. Through
patience and suffering, fill my heart
with faith and love.

June 7

O Holy Spirit! Give me joy that is unspeakable, love that passes knowledge, and peace beyond understanding.

June 8

You know my great need. Graciously draw near to me, and cover my head when I am in trouble. May the evils that the craftiness and subtlety of the devil or people work against me be brought to nothing by the goodness of your providence.

June 9

Almighty God! You know that I have no power to keep myself. If it is your will, keep me and those dear to me from all injury and illness that may happen to the body. Keep us from all evil that may attack and hurt the soul.

June 10

Teach me to pray, O Lord, as you taught your disciples, and direct my prayers so that I may wish for and ask only those things that are according to your will.

June 11

Remember me, Lord, now that you have come into your kingdom. Keep me true to you through this mortal life, and present me finally faultless before the presence of your glory with much joy.

June 12

You are my God, I will praise you. You are my God, I will exalt you. I will give thanks to you, for you are love and your mercy endures forever. Compelled by your kindness, I present myself to you a living sacrifice, holy and acceptable, which is my reasonable service.

June 13

*M*ay I not think too little of myself or too much, but soberly and rightly; and may I be and give to the world whatever you planned when you sent me into this world.

June 14

I am not my own but yours, my Master, by your creation, your providence, and your blood. May I always live as one who belongs – body, soul, and spirit – to the Lord.

June 15

O Holy Father! Make me humble and unselfish. Give me childlike faith to receive what you offer and to bear what you send. May a new sense of your presence and power, through the Holy Spirit, rest in me.

June 16

O true and living Vine, make me fruitful today with good works to do your will. You have given me a yearning for a holy life. Accomplish it by the grace of your Spirit dwelling in me and working through me day by day.

June 17

*G*ive me a pilgrim spirit. Enable me to be in the world but not of the world. Give me grace when selfish cravings war against my soul. May I always obey your heavenly calling.

June 18

*D*o not let me forget, O Lord, that the best and happiest life embraces the needs, sorrows, and trials of others. Give me closer sympathy with you, the one who did not please himself but whose life was continually laid down for others.

June 19

*G*uard me behind from the pursuit of my sins, and before from the attack of my foes. Lay your hand upon me to cover my head when I am threatened.

June 20

*T*ake away from me, I pray, O Father, the fear of people. May I fear you alone, with the fear born of love.

June 21

*M*y heart is weary, O God. The strain of life, the cruelty of the world, and the failure of human love have left me desolate. I fall at your feet. Do not be silent, lest I be like those who go down into the pit.

June 22

*K*eep my way, Heavenly Father, and fence me around with your protecting care, so that among all the changes and chances of life I may be defended by your gracious and ready help, through Jesus Christ my Lord.

June 23

*Y*ou know, Lord, how often I am badly hindered in running the race that is set before me. May your grace and mercy come to my help, so that I may finish my course with joy and receive the crown of life.

June 24

O blessed Lord, be the physician of my soul. Forgive its sins and heal its diseases. Lighten my heart with the knowledge of your truth, and grant me grace to pass through the remainder of this day, and of my whole life, to your honor.

June 25

*P*urify me, O God, by the fire of your Holy Spirit, so that I may please you with a pure mind and serve you with a chaste body.

June 26

*H*eavenly Father, send your Holy Spirit with the excellent gift of love, which is the bond of peace and holiness, so that I may love you with all my heart and soul and mind and strength, and my neighbor as myself.

June 27

*S*prinkle my heart, Heavenly Priest, from an evil conscience, and wash my life as with pure water, so that I may have boldness to enter within the veil and commune with God.

June 28

*S*pirit of Truth, help me to live with an unshuttered and uncurtained heart, of which the windows are ever open to the Holy City.

June 29

You are stirring up my nest, my Father; the old is changing and giving place to the new. Spread your wings beneath me and teach me to trust when I can see no earthly support to rest on.

June 30

You know, my Savior, how I wait for footsteps that do not come, long for sympathy that is withheld, knock at doors that do not open, and dread what tomorrow may bring. I shrink from the loneliness of life and the mystery of that unknown future that stretches away in the dark like a moor beyond the light of home. But nothing can separate me from you.

JULY

July 1

The mountain peaks of the life that I want to live call me, yet they seem too steep and high for me to reach. But, Lord, you have infinite compassion for my weakness. Accomplish in me the good pleasure of your will and produce in my life the good things you have taught me to love.

July 2

Help me, merciful High Priest, to pray for those who have met with accident and sudden sorrow; for those who are passing through fires, that they may not be burned; for those who are wading in deep waters, that they may not be swept down; for those who are surrounded by enemies, that they may not be overpowered; for those who are lonely, and desolate, and forlorn, that they may not lose heart.

July 3

O Lord, you are the brightness of your Father's glory and the exact image of his person. May I catch some of that light and reflect some of that image, so that people I meet may turn from the reflection to you, the eternal reality.

July 4

Help me not to faint under your chastenings and not to be discouraged by your rebukes. Help me to share your holiness.

July 5

*J*esus Christ who makes morning and evening rejoice, shed in my soul your light, and love, and life, so that I may be as pure and radiant as alpine heights at dawn, and noon, and evening.

July 6

*Y*ou, O Christ, are all I want. May your grace so overwhelm me that, having all sufficiency in all things, I may abound in every good work.

July 7

*F*ill me, Heavenly Father, with your grace, so that I may be enabled to walk in the good works that you have prepared for me.

July 8

*F*eed me, Lord, with your flesh and blood, according to your promise, for they are meat and drink indeed. May you live in me and I in you.

July 9

O true Vine of God, I want to abide in you so that your life passing through my life may bear much fruit for your glory.

July 10

Heavenly Father! Send the good news of your salvation to the ends of the earth. Be with your missionary-servants who are engaged in preaching the gospel. Turn the hearts of many people to Christ, and make them obedient to your truth.

July 11

*F*ather, hasten the time when all creation shall be delivered from the bondage of corruption to the glorious liberty of your children. May your purpose soon be accomplished in your church and in the coming of our Lord Jesus Christ.

July 12

O Lord, deliver me from terror of the night, and arrows that fly by day, from pestilence that stalks in darkness, and from destruction that wastes at noonday. Leaning on your strength, comforted by your grace, and guarded by your angels, may I live in peace and safety.

July 13

*G*racious Father! I yield to you my will and desires, my body and mind, the thoughts of my heart, and the longings of my spirit. Perfect, I pray, that which concerns me.

July 14

*M*ay I behold your glory, my God, until my face and life begin to reflect it, though I do not know it.

July 15

*F*ountain of Life, spring up in me! Light of Life, illumine me! Source and Sun of Love, pour your love in my heart by the Holy Spirit. Lamb of God, you are in the midst of the throne, and yet you tread the rough pathway of this world. Be my Shepherd!

July 16

*M*y Father, I know that you love me and that your love has chosen my path. I would have it so. Help me to be satisfied with your wise choice of rough and smooth, of time and tide, of sun and shower. May I finish my journey with joy.

July 17

Teach me to do your will, for you are my God; and if I begin by choosing it, may I end by delighting in and loving it.

July 18

Heavenly Father, I have been a wayward child, loving my own way and fretting too often against your appointments. Forgive me, I pray, and put away my sin.

July 19

Give me, Father, such faith in your fatherly love and mercy that I may never be concerned and troubled about the things of this life but seek the coming of your kingdom and your glory.

July 20

In your house, my Savior, there are many mansions! Do not let my heart be troubled, neither let it be afraid. Give me the Comforter and peace that no one can take away.

July 21

*B*ring near the day of your reign, O God, and hasten the coming of your kingdom, so that 'the mystery of lawlessness' may be brought to an end and all people confess Jesus Christ as Lord.

July 22

*H*ave mercy, I pray, on all who call themselves Christians; lead them out of their wanderings and divisions so that people may see their unity in Jesus Christ and believe that you sent him to be the Redeemer of the world.

July 23

*D*ear Lord, I am poor and weak! I have nothing worth giving to you. My best is defiled by sin. Take my bankrupt soul into eternal partnership with you and say to me, 'All that I have is yours.'

July 24

*H*elp me, Lord, to take up my cross and follow you in the path of your humiliation, so that I may at last see your face in righteousness and receive from you that crown that does not fade away.

July 25

*O*Lord Jesus, Captain of Salvation, who knows the workings of evil against my soul, save me, I pray, in temptations and trials. Make a way for me to escape, support me with your mighty power, and enable me to become more than a conqueror.

July 26

*M*ay I love you, my God and Father, not for what you give but for yourself, with a holy, absorbing, and increasing love.

July 27

I thank you, God, that your divine Son was given that He might destroy the works of the devil. Deliver me, I pray, from evil, and purify me even as Christ is pure.

July 28

*G*ive me grace, Heavenly Father, to be steadfast, unmovable, always flourishing in the work of the Lord.

July 29

*M*ost merciful Father!
I claim the fulfilment
of your covenant promise that you
would write your law upon my heart
and remember my sins no more.

July 30

*P*our down upon me, O God,
the richness of your mercy,
forgiving those things of which my
conscience is afraid, and giving me
those good things for which I am not
worthy to ask, through the merits
and mediation of Jesus Christ, my
Lord.

July 31

Keep me from fashioning you for myself, God my Savior, after my own imaginings. May I not make a graven image of you, but know you as you are.

AUGUST

August 1

King of Love, let the leaves of the Tree of Life be for my healing, and let your peace settle down, like the evening calm, on my harassed nature. Minister nourishment to the fainting and comfort to those who have failed; temper the gladness of success with the humility that gives the credit to you.

August 2

Lord God Almighty, how shall I ever thank you for adopting me into your family and making me one of your children. You have taught me to know you, talk to you, and love you. You are my shield and my very great reward. Bless me, and fill me with your Holy Spirit.

August 3

*L*et the 'great cloud of witnesses' who have gone before and entered into their rest be to me an example of a faithful life, and even now may I be refreshed with their joy and run with perseverance the remainder of the race that is set before me.

August 4

I pray, Heavenly Father, for those who are wandering from your ways in darkness and error. Have mercy upon them and turn them to yourself. Re-kindle in them the flame of your love, and restore them to joy, so that they may praise you for your recovering mercy.

August 5

*Y*ou know the wants and pity the infirmities of your people, O Lord. Give to us, out of your inex-haustible fullness, all the things we need.

August 6

*B*lessed Christ, do not let sin have dominion over me. If I have to pass through experiences in which the presence of sin is strong, do not let me give way to it. When I am fiercely tempted, do not let me yield.

August 7

*P*rosper, I pray, every great effort that seeks to promote peace, purity, sobriety, and justice in the world; and help me as I do small things. May I do them with a sincere desire to help others and to please you.

August 8

*L*et all things, O Lord, be begun, continued, and finished in you. Be the alpha and omega, the beginning and the end, of every year, month, day, hour, and moment of my life.

August 9

*L*et the fire of your love consume in me all sinful desires of the flesh and of the mind, so that I may more fully live in Jesus Christ my Lord. May I seek the things that are above where Christ is, seated at the right hand of God.

August 10

*H*eavenly Father, give me assurance of your protection in the troubles of my life. Keep me in quietness of spirit, always trusting in your care.

August 11

*M*ake me, my Father, faithful and steadfast, accomplishing the work of faith and labor of love that you have committed to my care, so that I may please you through Jesus Christ my Lord.

August 12

*Y*ou have given me gladness, Lord. Help me to make others glad and pass on to them the comfort with which you have comforted me. At whatever cost, may I have fellowship with you in your redemptive purpose and ministry.

August 13

*L*ord Jesus, show me each day
how I may serve with you in
opening blind eyes and in turning
men and women from darkness to
light and from the power of Satan to
God. May your kingdom come, your
power work through my hands, your
love throb in my heart.

August 14

*G*ive me wisdom, Lord, that I
may know what things I ought
to do; and give me grace and power
to do them.

August 15

*C*omforter of the comfortless, teach me to pray with you. Wherever there are broken hearts, heal them; captives, release them; smoking flax, fan its spark; bruised reeds, make them pillars in your temple.

August 16

*L*et me not be put to shame, my Lord, but make me love and fear you with all my heart, so that I may at last meet you with confidence and joy.

August 17

*T*rue and only Shepherd, give me grace so that I may never grieve your Holy Spirit or wander from your flock.

August 18

*A*ccomplish in me, O God, the desires of goodness that you have created in my heart, and perfect your work of faith, so that Jesus Christ may be glorified in me.

August 19

*H*ave mercy on me, most merciful Father, and, for the sake of Jesus Christ, forgive my sins and take away all waywardness. May I serve you in newness of life.

August 20

I thank you, Heavenly Father, that I know you in Jesus Christ our Lord. He is the brightness of your glory, the exact image of your person. In his face I see your face. I humbly ask that the Holy Spirit may open my eyes more fully to see, and my heart more eagerly to love, you in him.

August 21

O Lover of all, I pray for a blessing to rest on those in hospitals; on those who have suffered for a long time; on those who have the care of young children; and on those whose lot is in places where the light of your gospel does not shine.

August 22

M ake me sensitive to you, my Lord and Master, to hear your voice and receive your gracious words. May the Holy Spirit take the things that are yours and, through the Word, reveal them to me.

August 23

*D*ear Lord, you do not despair of the most ignorant and unworthy. Heal and save and teach me.

August 24

*C*aptain and Leader of the Holy War, may I take up the whole armor of God: having on the belt of truth, the breastplate of righteousness, the helmet of salvation, and the gospel of peace on my feet. May I take up the shield of faith. May I have no fellowship with unfruitful works of darkness, but reprove them with consistent life and faithful words.

August 25

*M*ay my heart be as a palace where peace abides. But do not let me miss whatever blessings may be gained or lessons learned from the fiery ordeals of life.

August 26

*Y*ou are the door, O Lord! Through you may I pass out to my daily work and back again to rest, and, whether in work or rest, may I abide in your safekeeping.

August 27

*F*or food and clothes, for strength and health, for friends and love, for the beauty of nature, for the ladder between our lives and heaven, for the privilege of prayer, for the open Bible, I thank you, God, and worship your name.

August 28

*W*e pray for this tired and feverish world; for those who do not know you; for little children; for all who suffer; for the absent, the lonely, the tired, the wayward, the sinful; for your servants who are about to faint in their service for you and for people, strengthen them, Father.

August 29

*W*hen the storms are high, Lord Jesus, may I feel you near; as when you came through the mist and across the storm-swept waves, saying, 'It is I. Be not afraid.'

August 30

O my Refuge, outside of you the waves are high and the winds fierce, but in you I have haven, protection, and peace. You are my pavilion, my refuge, my strong tower, the house of my defence, my shield, and my great reward.

August 31

*L*ord, I thank you for the pillar of cloud by day and of fire by night. May I never go in front or loiter behind. When it moves in the path of duty or suffering, help me to follow it; when it stays, teach me to gladly take and use the rest that you give.

SEPTEMBER

September 1

*M*y Savior, may I live in the spirit of prayer today. There is a life of which I sometimes get a glimpse, in which the heart goes out to you the whole day long – smiling to you in joy, confiding to you in sorrow, and talking with you about the details of my life. Graciously make such a life mine.

September 2

*Y*our church, Lord, languishes for want of refreshing. We are poor and needy. We seek water. We are thirsty. Create rivers in the hills and fountains in the valley. Make the wilderness a pool and the dry land a place of springs.

September 3

*O*Lord who has the key of David, who opens and no one can shut, who shuts and no one can open, go before me today, I pray, opening shut gates so that I may pass through them to fulfil your purpose in my life.

September 4

*H*eavenly Father, engraft your Son, Jesus Christ my Lord, in my heart, so that I may bear the fruit of holy living to the honor and praise of your name.

September 5

O Lord who loves with an ever-lasting love, cause your light and life and love to shine in my heart so that I may be transformed, and so that people may turn from me to worship you.

September 6

*G*ive me, Lord Jesus, the in-dwelling of your Spirit. May he guide me into all truth, according to your promise.

September 7

Y ou, God, are the giver of good and perfect gifts. To you I offer worship and praise, not only with my lips but by giving myself to your service and walking with you in righteousness all my days.

September 8

D o not leave me, nor forsake me in my toilsome climb. Help me to mount up with wings like eagles, to run and not be weary, to walk and not faint.

September 9

*L*et the Holy Spirit be to me a burning fire, consuming the waste and selfishness and suspicion of my heart, and kindling the pure flame of warm affection toward all who name the name of Christ in sincerity.

September 10

*L*ord Jesus, bring quickly the time of homecoming, when we shall no longer be strangers and pilgrims but enter into your heavenly city and meet again with loved ones, through the blood by which we are made whiter than snow.

September 11

*B*e not far from me, O Lord, this day; and through all its hours may I do those things that are pleasing in your sight. May I, like Enoch, walk with you.

September 12

*A*lmighty God, teach me the dignity of labor, the honor of work, the joy of being able to do something in the world. And help me to remember that, at my best, I am an unworthy servant. Forgive, I pray, my shortcomings and failures. Prosper and establish the work of my hands.

September 13

*B*lessed are you, Lord, for you daily carry my burdens and load me with benefits. You are the God of my salvation. Make me stand strong.

September 14

*M*y Savior, my heart is very broken as I think of all the sorrow and pain that I have given you. Let tears of gratitude mingle with those of remorseful grief, as I remember your patient, overflowing, unmerited love.

September 15

*F*ather of Jesus, give me that same Holy Spirit who raised him from the dead, so that he may raise me also. I long that Jesus Christ's risen life will be more evident in me.

September 16

*M*y Father, may the Holy Spirit enable me to realize in daily life my true position in Christ. Where he is, may I, in heart and mind, continually stay.

September 17

*L*ord, I pray that through your grace sin may be destroyed in me, and that through the power of your resurrection I may walk in newness of life.

September 18

O God, quickly send your Holy Spirit to the world, to convict people of sin and righteousness and judgment, so that many may be deeply affected. May times of refreshing come from your presence.

September 19

*H*oly Savior, make my life deeper, stronger, richer, gentler, more Christ-like, more full of the spirit of heaven, more devoted to your service and glory.

September 20

*B*lessed Jesus! Mercifully grant that I may follow the example of your patience. May I learn to wait for the Lord, to be strong, and to take courage.

September 21

*M*ost holy God, I rejoice that the Savior lives to intercede as our High Priest and Mediator. Through the torn veil let my prayers ascend to you, mingled with the fragrance of Christ's perfect merit, with which you are well pleased.

September 22

*D*ear Lord Jesus! I thank you that you love me. I am the least of saints and the chief of sinners, but in the bankruptcy of my soul I trust in the riches of your grace.

September 23

God of my fathers, thank you that life is a pilgrimage, that the earth is not my resting place, that every day brings me nearer my home in the city of God. Thank you that you are willing to be my companion in every step of my earthly pilgrimage.

September 24

Most gracious God! Help me, I pray, to be a good and kind influence on those whom I meet each day. May I reflect in look and gesture the sweet fragrance of Christ.

September 25

*T*ake my love, like the five barley loaves and two small fish, and multiply it, so that it may be pleasing to you and a blessing to others.

September 26

*H*oly Savior! I am often weary of myself, but I pray that you would not become weary of me. I am a broken reed and smouldering flax, but I pray that you would not become discouraged with me. Leave me not comfortless, but come to me.

September 27

*E*nable me, Lord, for your name's sake, to walk righteously and speak truly; to despise the gain of oppression and fraud; to keep my hands clean from unholy actions; to stop my ears from uncharitable and polluting talk; to shut my eyes from looking at evil.

September 28

O God of peace and righteousness, may peace reign among the nations of the earth and among the people of the earth. May war, slavery, impurity, blasphemy, drunkenness, and all other evils that deprave and injure humanity, cease. Your will be done, on earth as it is in heaven.

September 29

*H*eavenly Father! May I use well the discipline and testing through which I am passing. May I see your hand in every dark hour.

September 30

*G*reat High Priest, I come to you in confession and penitence. Do not deal with me according to my sins, do not reward me according to my failures. Teach me to hate evil and, by your grace, to flee from wrongdoing.

*O*CTOBER

October 1

*I*f I have loved darkness more than light, if I have left some brother or sister wounded by the way, if I have preferred my aims to yours, if I have been impatient and would not wait, if I have marred the pattern drawn out for my life, if I have cost tears to those I love, if my heart has murmured against your will, O Lord, forgive!

October 2

*E*nable me to do not only those things I like to do, but also what I ought to do. May I be guided not by feelings, but by conscience. May I be content with the boundaries that your providence sets. Cause me to be faithful in a little. In ordinary tasks may I learn your deep lessons of patience, trust, and faithfulness.

October 3

*F*ather, you have loved us, you still love us, and you will love us forever. Your love is beyond knowing. It is like a warm, sunlit ocean enwrapping the tiny island of my life. I bathe in it but can never reach its limit. I thank you for its depths and lengths.

October 4

*M*ay I delight myself in you, Almighty God. Put gladness in my heart, more than in the time when corn and wine increase. Teach me how great is your goodness and how great your beauty.

October 5

ive me grace to see the beauty lying at my feet in the commonplaces of life, to feel that you are near, and to find that life is as wonderful today as when men and women saw you in the days when you were on earth.

October 6

ear Lord, may I find a balm for my own griefs, and a solace for my own disappointments, in sympathy and ministry to those whose hearts are breaking around me. Give me a quick eye and skilful touch so that I may become like Barnabas, a source of consolation and encouragement.

October 7

*L*ord Jesus, you have revealed the Father; you have brought us near God. I thank you that I may look boldly at the glory of your eternal throne and know that all the attributes of God are on my side.

October 8

*L*ord Jesus, Savior! The storm is high and the night dark. Come to me, I beg you.

October 9

*M*ay I dwell in you, O Christ, and you in me, so that you may be magnified in my body, whether by life or by death. In the commonplaces of life may others see in me that which will remind them of you, my unseen Lord.

October 10

I ask you, Lord, to bless those whom I love. Minister to them as I would if I could be with them, and better than I would, because your thoughts and ways are so much more tender and helpful than mine could ever be. Keep them safe beneath your wing.

October 11

*T*ake me to your heart, Heavenly Father, and love me, though stained with toil, travel, and sin. Cover me with the robe of our Savior's righteousness.

October 12

*K*eep me this day from sin. Into your hand I commend my spirit. Live in me, Lord, by your good Spirit, so that my life may be full of helpfulness and generosity. Supply my daily needs. Help me to be a gracious, loving influence on those I meet today.

October 13

*T*he world is dear to you, Father. You sent your Son to save it. Send your Spirit to comfort and renew it. May he brood over the chaos, as he did of old upon the deep. May order and peace reign among all people. May Jesus come quickly to receive his bride.

October 14

*M*y Father, God! Enable me to roll my burdens on you, to trust you, and to believe that when I stand with you in perfect daylight I shall understand what now I take on trust.

October 15

For all who are in sickness and sorrow, for those who face this day with anxiety, for those who are called to suffer, to undergo special trials, to pass through the Valley of the Shadow, I humbly pray that they may be sustained.

October 16

Wonderful and gracious Father, I am tired with working, striving, thinking. I fall back on your love, tenderer than a mother's and lasting forever.

October 17

Divine Lord, when I am most absorbed in my necessary business, may your presence be constantly with me. May I be faithful to you in little things. May I follow the guidance of your Spirit until he leads me to the perfect day.

October 18

Heavenly Father, give us faith in your guardian care. May we realize that we are surrounded by hosts of watching angels. Bless and defend and save all whom we love. May we share together your heavenly blessing.

October 19

I want, O Lord, to take up your yoke and learn from you, for you are gentle and lowly in heart. Give me rest for my soul. Teach me to be joyful always in all things, to pray without ceasing, and in everything to give thanks.

October 20

I give thanks to you with my whole heart and sing praises to your name for your saving kindness and truth. Bless the Lord, O my soul, and all that is within me, bless his holy name. Hallelujah, for the Lord God omnipotent reigneth!

October 21

I pray for my companions in life's pilgrimage, for the feeble and the ready-to-halt, for the despondent and the oppressed, for the poor and sick and forlorn. May their valleys of weeping become filled with springs of joy.

October 22

O Light of Life, shine upon my heart that longs for the summer of your love. All the saints who gather around you in the world where night never comes find in you their true completion and perfect joy. Be to me what you are to them, and let me find in you the foretaste of heaven.

October 23

Undertake for the oppressed and weak, for slaves and prisoners. Watch by the bedside of the sleepless. Console the hearts of the bereaved. Hurry the coming of your kingdom and gathering of your elect.

October 24

Lord, you did illumine the heart of Thomas with the clear radiance of your risen glory, and you know how to deal with the doubts and perplexities of my heart. I have not seen, but give me the confidence of those who have believed.

October 25

*G*ive to me 'the hidden manna and the white stone.' May I become a pillar in your temple, inscribed with your own new name. May I be dressed in white clothes. Make me pure with your holiness.

October 26

*L*ord, give me to drink of the water of life, and let that spring of which you spoke rise in my heart to eternal life.

October 27

*O*n this new day I adore you, my God and Father. The light is your garment; the heavens are the curtain of your home; the clouds are your chariot; the winds, your messengers; the fire, your minister. Of you, and through you, and to you are all things.

October 28

*H*oly, holy, holy are you, O God! Heaven and earth are full of your glory. Every day is a day that you have made. May I be hungry no more, neither be thirsty anymore, because I am completely satisfied with you.

October 29

*C*ovenant-keeping God, your faithfulness reaches to the skies; help me to reckon upon it in every step of my life's pilgrimage. Your righteousness is like the great mountains; may I keep it before me always.

October 30

*M*y Master and Lord! May I know that you go before me as of old you went before your disciples. The sword pierces your heart before it touches mine, and the waves pound upon you before they reach me. The heavy part of my cross rests on you.

October 31

*M*ake me hate evil and cling to that which is good. Take from me my heart of stone and give me a heart of flesh. Deliver me from my idols. Take from me the love of sin. Put your Spirit within me, and cause me to walk in your way.

NOVEMBER

November 1

*G*racious Lord, forgive my past. Keep me as the apple of your eye. Surround me with your guardian care, and realize in me your highest purposes. Then I will offer in your tabernacles sacrifices of joy. I will sing, I will sing praises to the Lord.

November 2

I adore you, Holy Father! There is no limit to your power or to your love. You are greatly to be praised. You are greatly to be loved. There is none like you, majestic in holiness, awesome in glorious deeds, doing wonders. Accept the homage of my soul and life through Jesus Christ.

November 3

*O*God, make me increasingly conscious, I pray, of the indwelling of your Holy Spirit. May he bear witness with my spirit that, in spite of my sin, I am still your child. May he enable me to resist the temptations of the world, the flesh, and the devil.

November 4

*A*ccept what I have done for your church and your name, great Lord. Though it be little in the eyes of people, may you receive, bless, and increase it.

November 5

*M*ake your Word more and more precious to me, Lord. In your Word may I learn your truth and be changed by it. Seeing your face in this mirror, may I be transformed into your likeness.

November 6

*T*here are so many mysteries in the world and in human life, Father. My eyes are tired of straining into the dark. Enable me to see you always. Refresh my eyes and heart as the rain refreshes the parched earth.

November 7

*Y*ours, Lord, is the greatness, and the power, and the glory, and the victory, and the majesty. All that is in heaven and on earth is yours. You are exalted King above all.

November 8

*G*racious, holy Savior! Cleanse my tears, purify my repentance, refine my hope, and accept me as needy and helpless. I can claim nothing, but I come to you because you have invited all who are weary and heavy-laden to come.

November 9

*H*oly Savior, keep our failures from leading us to be despondent and our successes from creating pride. Make right what is wrong. Undo what is harmful. Establish, strengthen, and prosper the work of our hands.

November 10

*L*ord Jesus, teach me how to apply the heavenly truth of your risen life to the ordinary things of my daily life. May I consider nothing common or unclean. May every ordinary bush be aflame with God.

November 11

Keep me, Lord, from sin today. May my behavior be ordered by your will. In all things may I do what is pleasing in your sight.

November 12

Heavenly Father! Do not deal with me as my sins, negligencies, and ignorances deserve. Wash my soiled soul and dirty garments. Forsake not the work of your hands. Perfect that which concerns me. Your mercy endures forever.

November 13

*F*ather, put all my sins behind you into the depths of the sea. Deliver me from the dominion and love of sin. Cover me with your grace, so that I may have strength for all things and thrive in every good work.

November 14

*E*ternal God! As my outward life decays, may I inwardly be renewed day by day. May my light affliction, which is but for a moment, work out for me a far greater and eternal weight of glory.

November 15

*L*ord Jesus, I pray for your one church, the members of which are scattered in many different churches and over the wide world. All who belong to you belong to each other. Grant that our love may be shown and confessed so that others might believe that the Father sent the Son.

November 16

*T*he good that I want to do, I do not do; the bad that I don't want to do, I do. I am sorry for my temper, my pride, my self-will, the hurtful thoughts I permit, the unkind, rash things I say! But you knew all this about me before you called and saved me.

November 17

*T*ake me as I come home to you, soiled and dusty with the sin and business of the day. Wash me from unrighteousness, purifying and making clean every part of my life.

November 18

*H*eavenly Father, I thank you for the gift of your Son, who is the pearl of great price, the hidden treasure that makes the soul rich forever, the delight of heaven, the glory of his church, the all-sufficient portion of his people.

November 19

*O*ur Father, bring quickly in all lands the reign of your Son. May all rulers fall down before him, all nations serve him. Let his name endure forever and all people be blessed in him.

November 20

*T*each me, O Lord, the way of your commands, and enable me to keep them to the end. Give me understanding and delight in all your law.

November 21

When temptations attack me today, do not let me distrust your leading hand, nor think that failure is inevitable, nor concern myself too much with the great adversary. Be with me in the struggle. Let your angels minister to me.

November 22

Hear my prayer for our rulers and country, for all who exercise authority, or enact laws, or pronounce judicial decisions. Enlighten those who teach, or write books, or edit newspapers. Give peace in our time, Lord, I pray.

November 23

*F*orgiving Savior! If I have in my heart anything against my brother or sister, may I have the grace of silence concerning it to others and the grace of speech about it to him or her alone. Let the love that covers a multitude of sins be mine.

November 24

*H*oly Father, I mourn the disagreements that divide your people and ask you to fulfil our Lord's prayer that the people whom he purchased by his blood may all be one, even as you, our Father, are in him and he in you.

November 25

*B*lessed is the one whose strength is in you, my God, and in whose heart are your ways. May my strength be yours perfected in my weakness. May my heart be strong to hope, to love, and to endure.

November 26

*S*trong Son of God, you are like the sun going forth from his chamber and rejoicing as a strong man to run his race. Gather me up into fellowship with you in your strength and pity, and in your tenderness toward the weary and weak.

November 27

*T*o you, heavenly Father, I commend my fellow-workers on every part of life's battlefield. Let no defeat discourage them. Let no sudden temptation overcome them. Let no long-continued sorrow wear out their loyalty or discourage their faith.

November 28

*M*aster, draw me aside into sympathy with you in your ceaseless prayers for your church and the world. Let it not be enough for you to pray for me; pray in me.

November 29

*O*Lord who hears prayer, may I pray in faith and confidence that you will hear and answer.

November 30

*T*hough my outward life be a desert march, may my heart live in the heavenly places where Christ, the forerunner, has entered. May I eat of the fruit of the land, and drink of the river of God, and triumph over everything that opposes.

*D*ECEMBER

December 1

*M*y Savior and Example! I pray for others – for those who misunderstand and injure me, for any I have wronged, for those to whom I have been a stumbling block, for such as might have been saved if I had been more faithful. Do for them by other means what I might have done.

December 2

*F*orbid, Heavenly Father, that I should ever lose the freshness and beauty that you can maintain in the hearts of your children. May it be true of me today, during the stress of many tasks, that I have a lovely spirit.

December 3

*F*or all your gracious care, I thank you. Help me to trust in your infinite love, especially when things happen that try me and fill me with sorrow and even bitterness. May these trials wean me from all that grieves you.

December 4

O Savior, forgive my sins, my faithless tears, and my complaints. Forgive my thought-lessness of others and my self-centered anxiety. Support me with your love. May I experience richer fellowship with you.

December 5

*G*reat Shepherd! Lead me in pastures of tender grass and by cool waters of rest. But if my way lies in rocky and desert places, go before me with your goodness. May your rod and staff be my comfort.

December 6

*H*urry your coming, Lord Jesus, to right the wrongs of time and establish your everlasting kingdom. Let me, though most unworthy, sit with you at your table and see you in your glory.

December 7

*H*ow great is your goodness, dear God, which you pour out upon those that love you, which you lavish upon those that trust you. Of you, and through you, and to you are all things, and to you shall be glory and honor forever.

December 8

*L*ord Jesus! May my heart affirm good things and my mouth speak of our King. May my conversation be graceful, seasoned with salt, full of truth and love.

December 9

You make your home, O God, with those who are of a humble and contrite spirit and who love your Word. Take my weakness into your strength, my ignorance into your wisdom, my changefulness into your constancy.

December 10

Gracious Father, I thank you for the Son of your love, for all that he has done for us, and will do; for all that he has been to us, and will be. I thank you that he holds us in his strong, pierced hand and loves us with love that will not let us go.

December 11

*M*y Father! Teach me to trust your love. May I cling to it when the dark clouds brood, as well as when the sun shines. May I never doubt that what you are doing for me is best, and that what I do not know I shall know some day.

December 12

*G*reat God, I am common earthenware, but clean, purify, and fill me with springs of living water that will overflow from my life to refresh parched and weary hearts.

December 13

*G*reat God of all! I pray for the world, especially for those who in distant lands are sowing the precious seed of your gospel. Bless them in their work, and encourage them when their hearts are faint.

December 14

*H*oly Spirit, may my heart be filled with your love, my lips with gentle, helpful words, and my hands with kind, unselfish deeds. May those who see me know that I have been with Jesus.

December 15

I humbly ask, O Christ, that your peace may be the garrison of my heart, with its affections, and of my mind, with its thoughts. May your peace reign in me, and out of this peace may I serve.

December 16

*G*iver of peace! Give peace to this house, peace to the homes of my friends and neighbors, peace to all tired workers, lonely pilgrims, and sin-weary hearts, peace to your church so that her schism and discord may end. Your peace, heavenly Father!

December 17

You have taught us to look for the time when creation shall be made free with the glorious liberty of the sons of God. Bring soon that day, Lord, when your own hand shall wipe tears from our faces, and former things shall have passed away.

December 18

Gracious Lord, may your Holy Spirit fill my heart with the sense of your nearness and loving fellowship. Order my steps in your way, and then walk with me. Teach me to do the things that please you.

December 19

*F*ather! My heart is alarmed by the storm and strife of life. Be with me. May my soul enter the Sabbath rest that is promised to the people of God.

December 20

*G*reat Burden-bearer, I bring to you my anxieties and cares – about myself and my dear ones, about my body and soul, about the things of this life and those of eternity. I cannot carry them. They rob me of peace and strength. Take them, heavenly Father, and carry them for me.

December 21

*D*ear Savior, you sent us the Comforter. For the temptations that he has overcome in us, for the comfort he has given us, for the fruit he has produced in us, for the glimpses of your love he has shown us, and for the hopes he has inspired in us, I thank you.

December 22

*G*reat God! Teach me the art of so living in fellowship with you that every act may be a psalm, every meal a sacrament, every room a sanctuary, and every thought a prayer. May the bells that ring to common duty be inscribed with 'Holiness to the Lord.'

December 23

*L*ord, may all uncleanness and filthiness, foolish talking, covetousness, bitterness, wrath, and anger be put away from me, with all malice. May I forgive as God in Christ has forgiven me.

December 24

*B*ring quickly the coming of your kingdom, and to this end bless the efforts of your workers the world over. May the kingdoms of this world become the kingdoms of our God and of his Christ. Help me to work for the coming of that day.

December 25

O God who sent forth your Son, may the purity, simplicity, and beauty of the holy child, Jesus, be poured like a sweet fragrance through our hearts and lives. Bless the absent and those we love on this Christmas day. Bless the lonely and the sick and the destitute. May we all meet in the great homecoming.

December 26

*S*avior, I commend to you those whom I have injured, or spoken against, or failed to help. I pray for those who have treated me wrongfully and despitefully. I intercede for my family and friends, for sufferers and mourners, and for all your saints everywhere.

December 27

*B*lessed Lord, may I be strong not for myself alone, but for others. Teach me to bear the infirmities of the weak, to support those that are overborne in the fight of life, and to lighten the load of care beneath which many of my fellow-believers are pressed to the earth.

December 28

*H*oly Spirit, make me merciful in my judgment of others. May I think no evil. Deliver me from the spirit of retaliation. Help me to speak and think of others as I would have them do of me. Make me pure in heart, not only in my outward walk but in my deepest thoughts.

December 29

*M*ay I be kept, gracious Master, from the corruption that is in the world through lust. May my speech be always with grace, seasoned with salt. May my behavior be becoming to the gospel of Christ. May there be nothing in my loneliest moments to cause you shame.

December 30

O Head of the church, I pray for all who minister your gospel. Enrich them with knowledge and speech. As they break the living bread, may they themselves be nourished. As your living water flows through them to others, may it keep their hearts fresh and fruitful.

December 31

Y ou have brought me, gracious God, through the year. Accept my thanks. I trust you for what you have withheld as I bless you for what you have given. May goodness and mercy follow me throughout the remaining days of my life and bring me at last to the house of the Lord, where I shall be with you forever.

MORNING
EVENING

DAILY READINGS BY
C.H. SPURGEON

Morning & Evening

Daily Readings

C. H. Spurgeon

A wealth of Biblical teaching from Spurgeon. He meditates on two portions of scripture each day with applications that are very relevant for contemporary Christians. Spurgeon's characteristically pithy comments hit home with a wit and elegance rarely found in other writing. Spurgeon was, primarily, a pastor and this shows with the concern he shows here for the hearts of the reader. Christians, young and old, will find his comments challenging, stimulating and direct. This edition is in a high quality diary style finish, with a gilt page edging, a presentation page and a bookmark.

This is the most complete and unabridged version available of the best-selling Morning and Evening devotions. The luxury finish makes an excellent gift for a business associate, graduate or relative.

ISBN 978-1-84550-013-9 (Matt Black)
ISBN 978-1-84550-014-6 (Matt Burgundy)
ISBN 978-1-84550-015-3 (Matt Tan/Burgundy)
ISBN 978-1-84550-183-9 (Matt Tan/Blue)

CHEQUE BOOK
OF THE
BANK OF FAITH

DAILY READINGS BY
C.H. SPURGEON

Chequebook of the Bank of Faith

Daily Readings

C. H. Spurgeon

A short reading for every day. Spurgeon wrote this selection of readings to encourage believers to enter into the full provision that their relationship to Jesus entitled them to realise, on a daily basis. He explains we have to present the promises of Scripture to God in prayer and faith, anticipating that he will honour what he has said.

ISBN 978-1-84550-070-2 (Matt Tan/Green)
ISBN 978-1-84550-071-9 (Matt Tan/Burgundy)

IN GREEN PASTURES

Devotional Readings For Every Day Of The Year

J.R. MILLER

In Green Pastures

Devotional readings for every day of the year

J.R. Miller

J R Miller (1840-1912), considered by many the most popular and gifted devotional writer of his era, leads us through our daily meditations, displaying his amazing gift for drawing and expounding on Gods word.

Simple, accessible and tender this is a wonderful devotional book that will enhance your quiet time, and serve as a valuable source of inspiration and guidance. Miller offers a wealth of practical wisdom for our everyday lives, challenging us to seek to follow Christ's example every day of the year.

ISBN 978-1-84550-032-0

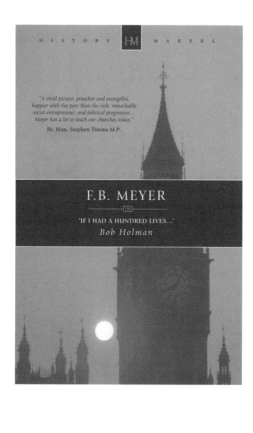

"A vivid picture: preacher and evangelist,
happier with the poor than the rich; remarkable
social entrepreneur; and political progressive...
Meyer has a lot to teach our churches today."
Rt. Hon. Stephen Timms M.P.

F.B. MEYER

'IF I HAD A HUNDRED LIVES...'
Bob Holman

F. B. Meyer

If I Had a Hundred Lives...

Bob Holman

On F. B. Meyer's death in 1929 The Daily Telegraph called him 'The Archbishop of the Free Churches'. The New York Observer noted that *'He has an international fame and his services are constantly sought by churches over the wide and increasing empire of Christendom.'* To the secular press of his time he was a key player on the world scene – yet this is the first chronological account of Meyer's life. Meyer was the minister one of Britain's first 'megachurches'. He was friends with D. L. Moody and ministered on both sides of the Atlantic. Mirroring in America what D. L. Moody was able to undertake in the U.K. He came from a conventional, middle class Victorian background and experienced no dramatic conversion. He was not a distinguished scholar or dramatic orator. His slight figure and retiring manner meant that he did not stand out in a crowd. Yet he drew crowds by the thousands, wrote books, which sold by the millions, and attracted working class people. The range of Meyer's activities is astonishing: preacher, pastor, writer, social activist, free church leader, Baptist president, advocate for missionary work and more. In his last years, he declared, 'If I had a hundred lives, they should be at Christ's disposal.' At times, it seemed as though he was living a hundred lives!

Bob Holman was Professor of Social Policy at Bath University. He continues to write a weekly column in The Herald. Now 'retired' he is still active as a visiting Professor at Glasgow and Swansea Universities.

ISBN 978-1-84550-243-0

Christian Focus Publications

publishes books for all ages

Our mission statement –

STAYING FAITHFUL

In dependence upon God we seek to help make His infallible Word, the Bible, relevant. Our aim is to ensure that the Lord Jesus Christ is presented as the only hope to obtain forgiveness of sin, live a useful life and look forward to heaven with Him.

REACHING OUT

Christ's last command requires us to reach out to our world with His gospel. We seek to help fulfil that by publishing books that point people towards Jesus and help them develop a Christ-like maturity. We aim to equip all levels of readers for life, work, ministry and mission.

Books in our adult range are published in three imprints.

Christian Focus contains popular works including biographies, commentaries, basic doctrine and Christian living. Our children's books are also published in this imprint.

Mentor focuses on books written at a level suitable for Bible College and seminary students, pastors, and other serious readers. The imprint includes commentaries, doctrinal studies, examination of current issues and church history.

Christian Heritage contains classic writings from the past.

Christian Focus Publications Ltd,
Geanies House, Fearn, Ross-shire,
IV20 1TW, Scotland, United Kingdom
info@christianfocus.com

www.christianfocus.com